MAGIC WORDS

POEMS

poems for millennials, makers and mothers

MAGIC WORDS

"You won't believe it, strange as it sounds
Extraordinary magic follows you around"

- *Ben Rector, Extraordinary Magic*

author's note

Some of these poems mention sensitive topics like miscarriage, postpartum depression, body image, overall mental health.

Please take care of yourself and skip if needed. <3

dedicated

to all millennial mothers doing the work, i see you.

table of contents

millennial

'81-'96

How many times have
we had to flip, regroup
pivot, reinvent,
for the sake of finding passion
and paying rent.

We're master artists
of creating our own
paths, stories, that no
one but us can tell,
because no one but us
has gotten us here.

Makeshift

Folding chairs unpacked -
side-by-side -
to create a makeshift couch
until the spirit moves/credit allows
the real thing.

A worn blanket as curtains
to block the sight(s) of neighbors,
a warm one to make this 'couch'
resemble cozy.

That gift of a slow cooker box as a
nightstand - don't bump!
the lamp will fall - but otherwise
a good (safe? unsure) idea.

Dusty leftovers - a desk - a shelf -
forgotten from the lives who stayed
here before we paid to.

These don't fit me
or my aspired-to-be,
but we're newlywed at 23
and can't say no to free shit.

Makeshift, for now, as we
swiftly begin our very real life.

Today

My brain says it's time to be sad,
but I did that yesterday.

Today I want to feel sunshine,
say hello to a bird.

I want to drink iced coffee
and sit on a quiet park bench
for seven minutes - it'd be heaven.

Today I want to meet a new friend,
because we both grabbed for
the same book at the library.

I want to trust myself.
Have fun and like myself.

Let today be all that.

Yours No More

My body was not truly mine
from 17-29.

My religion preached (a temple)
My fertility decided (miscarriage)
My depression promised (never enough)

Those who should have loved me
no matter what (size) threw
'concerns' shaped like judgements
at shapes that changed naturally.

I spent years reclaiming
myself, with more tattoos,
more food, more celebration,
less mileage, less hiding,
less expectation.

Pr(a)ying eyes have no hold
on me, I am free.

My body is yours no more.

The lazy summer sun reminds
me to shine without pressure
of overdoing it.

More of the good stuff

More sparkly bonfires as the sun sits low
More cherries and apples and pies made of both

More wishing on stars only split-second-seen
and five hour road trips because you missed me

More family dance parties in kitchens unkept
More cats cuddling gently into our necks

More novels and journals bursting their seams
More trips to the market and climbing tall trees

More singing our songs, nights out way too late
More yeses feeling right and nos that feel great

texting with old friends

HAPPY BIRTHDAY!
texts fly in, after morning
routines and the kids get to school.
THANKS! MISS YOU!

Back and forth,
it's been too longs.
I hope you're wells.
I WISH:
we were closer.
we could hang out.
give you a big hug.
DITTO!

I can't help but wonder
how old friendship would flourish if
we came back to one town,
up the street, same school, same team,
not fifteen years and three states away.

Who would us be now,
if we had at 34
what we had at 18.

LOVE YOU, TALK SOON!

Tens

I like the decades.
They carry both finality
and newness.
A series of memories
has ended
right in time for a fresh
batch to begin.
Giving us time to
grow and fail
and reflect.
But not long enough to
get buried.

1989 babies reclaim their childhood joys

At six we had our Barbies
And eight, American girls
At ten we loved to Skip-It
And twelve, Spice was our World

At fourteen we found Myspace
And fifteen, Taylor Swift
At seventeen we boldly said
I'm too cool for all of this

So we stopped it, and we dropped it
And rolled it under the bed
We left for strange new places
To be someone else instead

The great big world came knocking
With bills and work by nine
We yearned for days of simple fun
To perhaps go back in time

Then thirties brought back Barbie
And nonstop Taylor Swift
Flashbacks of our former selves
Swirled by like needed gifts

So reclaim joys of childhood
my friends, they're here to stay
Grown up and feeling like ourselves
with freedom and permission to play

Sleepyhead

I don't want to dream about you
anymore.

It was nice, at first.
Nostalgic, comfortable.

But being so close,
night after night,
brings a little too much
loneliness back to a place
I was sure I'd since filled.

Nearly half my years
since I've seen you,
but you're still familiar,
up in my sleepy head.

You should go. Or stay.
You don't feel far either way.

always someday, never now
too tired, too done
exhausted before it's begun

One More Thing

I would go to bed,
but productivity calls,
even at 11:45pm.

Read one more page,
or 20, I'm really behind
(my self-imposed goal
of 100 books a year).

Write one more line more,
or four. Find that word.

Remember yesterday,
prep one more thing
for tomorrow,
my brain is a waste, put
it away.

I'm fine. It's fine.
The millennial urge
to get one more thing done.
To get one thing right.

Summer Soiree

Dreamy pink clouds
linger over our lake.
Floats drifting slow,
making their own play.

Colors of coral in every
sun-dipped space,
with sparkles surrounding
your toes in the bay.

Reflections so bright,
we have much to say,
the wind gently blows as
we slow down the pace.

With sunset upon us,
we put things away.
Our old folding chairs
clink right into place.

The summer of soulmates,
a kiss on your face.
We'll never forget these
days of escape.

More Me

Coffee drips from
the old french press
like rain on a waiting day.

What am I - impatient, yes -
a little cold, warmed
by brew, good reviews,
an unexpected sunrise.
INFP, but pumpkin season
and light Styles can bring
smiles right out of me.

I grab my mug,
freshly new up to the rim,
press the record, listen,
drink 'til I'm more me.

3 rituals to keep the scaries at bay

Buy yourself the plant, the coffee
the flowers, the dress - you are
worth all of it (and more, like
deep love and trust) (but generous
gifts that make you smile matter, too)

Read your most cherished poem,
love note, fortune - letter from Grandma
or world-shifting teacher.
Let the words settle into your soft areas
and keep you tethered on unruly days.

Fill your mug, cup, tumbler with
your ideal brewed beverage - iced,
or calm - or spicy, ready to fully wake you.
Leave room for oat milk, new adventures
and all green lights on your commute.

As You Roll Into 30
   -for my little sister

Make your bed, and
make mornings slow,
drip coffee, a lap cat,
sun beams on the welcome mat.

Trust the process, and
process in thick journals
carried home from worlds away,
heal and change, your words may.

Be unforgettable, and
don't forget to breathe,
rest your maker hands, soul
so each day can start whole.

Be yourself, and
wonder at the bees,
caring, community, hive,
take note of where you thrive.

Embrace a new decade, and
let the newness lift you into
fresh joy, kindness, smiles.
Most of all, stay wild.

Light

Shining,
leading the way
through dark + hallway,
tunnel + trees,
murky emotions.

Be a light,
(bulbs don't last forever)
Clink, pop, out.
Replace with care.
Back to bright.

When again your
light goes out,
you know
how to set it aglow
once more.

Unfocus

I chew my straws
bite my nails

pick at my sweater's loose threads
fly through over/under 100 books
in the name of my "yearly goal"

I focus on anything
to distract from everything

11 Years

I wish we still converged
at the points that make
sense and bring us joy, but
we're recently practiced
at only meeting in tension
over silly things. I wish we
moved together, intertwined,
not parallel bodies in our
own lanes. I wish we could
reunite among memories of
more, adventure, love, but we
stay sitting at opposite ends on
the couch. I wish you and I meant
us, but these days it feels like
being alone, together.

talk to you later
yeah, like six months from today
not much will have changed

nostalgia

please refrain from
asking me to be present.
i don't want new memories.

please let me burrow into
my pink unicorn bedroom
and quietly live in that lost/
beloved little world a while.

i won't be there forever.

maker

Bound

Wrap your mind around
the ideas you dreamed.

You imagined
new and worthy things,
with a full heart and
fresh notebook page.

Make them known.

Believe
yourself.

They are bound
(by paper,
and certain)
to mean something.

Make a Mark

Can't keep my fingers from
the motion of a brush, a pen,
a marker. Even a crayon,
if that's all I can find.

Make a mark.
Daubs and dots scattered through
blobs of collected color.
Swirls, silhouettes and splats.

Intertwined lines of
imaginary worlds, tucked in layers
of pigment and vision and water.

I'm not a master, but I'm here
anyways, always,
to make and leave a mark.

Talent/Dedication*

Talent is around, exists,
but if not activated, sits
unused.
Talent is helpful.
Talent is given.

Dedication is intentional.
Masterpieces are fought for
by messy hands, learning,
never stationary, emotions flailing.

The joy of the process must be
found in trials, in repetition,
in mistakes.
Fail. Make. Fall. Begin again.

*An artist needs both.

Words Could Never

My overflowing sketchbooks
(pages and towers)
reveal more about my life
than my mouth ever will.

Scratchy marks pile up when
I can't decide the next step.
(of life, today, last week, ever)

Meandering, muted colors
fill me with a quiet stillness
after an upside down week.

Dotted layers, a portrait
of what I wish
(I, life, the world) could be.

My overflowing sketchbooks
(volumes and stacks)
catch and process every feeling
my words could never explain.

Who Knows

My hands swiped
vibrant paint from tubes,
spread it and made a mess
until the covered canvas
transformed ~
worth looking towards.

Your eyes missed it
at first,
but good taste rushed in.
You absorbed
the treasured marks,
sensing, seeing
notes of love I layered
into the textures.

Your face shows
that you know
you're the only one
who knows.

I Want to Create in the Quiet

To make the best thing
I've ever dreamed, and tell no one.

I'll know it is worthy -
without asking anyone's opinion,
or waiting for fake yeses
to tell me what I do is real.

A decade of learning the tags,
beating the algorithm,
creating for double taps and
hearts that don't really love me at all.

A decade of always feeling
one step behind.

I'm tired of making content.
I only want to make to feel content.

All & Ever

Put your mind to it
doesn't work when my mind
wanders at a moment's notice.

It's all. It's ever.
It's creating in thick notebooks
and blending paint colors around
perfect pictures.

It's free. It's flying.
Running around the shelves
of various grocery stores
and libraries, only kind of knowing
what it needs.

It's jumping between emails,
tripping over toy towers,
raging around traffic,
and winding through dry vines
I haven't watered in I can't
remember how long.

How can I put my mind to it
if it never - even once in
it's life - has been still?

Collecting Colors

I borrowed pink from the dahlias
and grabbed orange and coral
from the lazy summer sun.

I threw in a muted yellow,
found over on my tomato leaves
that didn't survive.
(It added a nice dimension.)

I found green in the weeds,
near the overgrown blueberry bush.
Blue - let me pick that.
Make sure blackish-purple hits
the palette, too.

Collecting colors wherever I go,
to twist into shades
nature is already familiar with,
but my canvas is only just meeting.

The Chase

I see your bursting
sketchbook pages
and I know:
we are the same.

Chasing the art.

Critiquing ourselves
over every mark
and shade and pattern.

We race to catch the fate
of a color, battle to snatch
the moment of inspiration,
strive to place the perfect
paint proportions,

but where do we run
to know we belong?

Gemini and I

Gemini and I don't get along,
even though I am her.

I bring a list, she knocks it
from my hand, confidently.

I focus, she bursts out loud.

Gemini and I are too much,
sometimes, too wild to make
the most normal tasks flow.

I shout to the sky,
demanding that it fixes things,
(which is not how I envisioned
adulthood).

Full moon, my friend, I'll take
whatever help you have to share,
shimmer your wisdom down to me.

Gemini, June.
I'm sorry I called you
too much. Stay much.

not even hobbies can escape
my anxiety, she said, as she picked up
her fifth comfort project of the weekend

Piles

My cluttered
desk piles -
ranging from
done to
what is this again?

New ideas,
undeveloped,
inviting.

A sketched out mess
of mistakes and solved
mysteries.

Finished work,
ready for home.

Piles
and piles,
on my shelves,
in my
brain
are begging to
be sorted

so that someone else
can make sense of it
when I get lost
forever
underneath.

The Possibilities of a Blank Page

An empty notebook,
composition
yet to be discovered,
filled with
endless, beautiful
possibilities,
waiting with anticipation,
(and if you do it right,
a favorite new piece.)

Pick wisely.
Create correctly,
Don't waste this perfectly
clean canvas.
Process is key.

Overthink it
too much and the paper
will always stay blank.

silence is not nothing to say

no voices but
tap the pink pen
until the ink sends
dreams down the spine
onto the page line
no volume but
with writing we mend
to find peace again
our souls recombine
with ideas of kind

I told my brain to
calm down, but it only heard
'more coffee, we're good'.

mother

Same/Not

For five years I was
different from you.
Not a mother.

Until the end of July
when my body
finally said Yes.

Instantly alike.
Back in common.
Friendship resumed.

Until the end of September.
My loss, alone,
once again,
not a mother.

(How) Can we still be friends?

Rainbows
brought you down
to earth and
my head is
floating on clouds,
happy because
you are healthy
and you are here.

"I can't do this.

Don't leave me here alone
with him for another day."
I plead through week three
postpartum tears of dread.

You call in sick,
and sit by our side,
solid in emotions,
heavy with help,
and the rest is
supportive husband history.

what it feels like to become a mother

It's like all your
untouchable fears
that have been burrowed away
for years (deep into elbows
and heart valves
and the bottom of your belly)
burst forth with wild vigor
and begin to live on this side
of your eyes
so everyone (and you)
will knowlearndiscover
exactly what will break you open,
exactly what has changed your heart.

Postpartum Identity Crisis

This isn't what I dreamed of
I'd hoped I could remain
A portrait of my former self
To hold onto my name

Could no one think to tell me?
My identity would change
Instead of joining gracefully
So tangled we became

New mother plus her baby
Anxiety held reign
Giving care for twenty four
Depression timed the same

Will this all last forever?
I want to run away
I'm stronger than I think I am
So I'm clinging tight to stay

what old ladies say to a young lady after she has a baby

So beautiful!
Aren't you just loving this?
they preach, surrounding
a new mom and her
1/3/6/9 month old

Time moves so fast.
Everyday is such a gift.
Don't blink, enjoy every minute!

They offer
pressure-filled words,
as if these are new ideas,
as if she needs to hear them
to survive,
but what if what she really needs
is a nap.

Steps

I asked for you, promise.
Truly felt ready, but
stepped in with the wrong foot.

Fighting daily through fear.
Lost to the depths
of overwhelm and anger.

Then my feet landed.
I was finally standing still to see
help had always been there.

Our learning quickly steadied,
and gentle rain refreshed,
calming us for the first time.

Both our hearts grew,
hope came day by day,
and we walked in step together.

Wishy Washy

Brushed watercolor memories
ripple past my eyes.

I wish your year one was clearer.

Looking back now,
at least the layers
make it seem like
a vibrant period in our lives.

Even if, in the moment,
it was mostly wishy-washy.

Magic Words

are floating across
my waffles, coffee,
morning table.

How'd you sleep?
You're my favorite!
This is yummy.
What did you dream about?
(a monkey dancing on the moon
and a giraffe that eats donuts!)

Magic means different
things to different people.
Right now, you are
the most magic of all.

Partner Vision

You see the brightness
lightness and hope
of everything I don't

You know the joy,
worthiness of hard days
where I only stay away

You find meaning
in every interaction
while I see distractions

You are my clear eyes,
the bright side of my
anxious heart.

Just a Minute

I need a minute
turned half hour
half day
My head's full
of sad, it's all in
our way

Give me a minute
turned one
weekend away
So I have more
time to clear
this sad away

Wait till you see
I will be
night and day
I just need a
minute and
I'll be ok

you give me kisses
little, sweet on my forehead
you smile and i smile

Might be Magic

A bright, windy morning
Hot tea, light dapples, a book
Quiet except birds and the mail truck
Might be magic

A sun-soaked afternoon
Swings, soccer, popsicles
Loud with happiness and/or skinned knees
Might be magic

A crisp, easy evening
Grilled up, smoky, satisfied, together
Murmuring memories of the day
It's all magic

Trying/Better

I'm trying to take
care of myself.

Sometimes the two
other hearts in my home
come first.

Sometimes my brain
says, not today,
so sorry, friend.

I can only do my best, but
why can't that be better?

ways to say goodnight

"Love you, see you in the morning!"
I close my son's door,
he calls for one hug more.

"Love you babe, sleep well."
My husband rolls over,
I cuddle up to his shoulders.

"Shut your fucking brain off."
I stare, my eyes open wide
on the clock, one fifty nine.

Superhero

The leaves are dancing,
having fun, while
we do the same.

Chalk cities on outside
cement bloom bigger
as minutes go by.

You tinker at your trucks,
world-unaware,
lost in your very own.

Leaves and love swoop
in brisk wind, like
superheroes in the sky.

I marvel at your
face marveling at it all.

i told my son my plants can talk
so he thinks i'm talking to them
and not to myself

Mothering in February

Freezing at the playground
while my kid plays pirate ship.
He wants my attention,
but I have no joy to give.
I'm sad and verging hangry,
overwhelmed beyond my bones.
My ears are slapped by frigid air,
I wish that we were home.
This winter season stripped me
of the choice of being fun.
My brain feels twenty places
but I can't quite pinpoint one.

&, to.

Cluttered room,
front yard overgrowing,
sink overflowing…
They can wait.

I have coffee to drink
& sunshine to soak
snuggles to give
& rivers to float

birds to feed
& doodles to make
bubbles to pop
& ceilings to break.

Never Only

It's not accurate to
call you my only child.

I was a mother before you,
but they flew away,
known for nine weeks.

Then you shone,
my rainbow, bright,
and I was mother once more.

By quick sight,
(strangers,
knowing none of our
history, think)
you're my only,
but we remember.

Three with dad.
Four with angel.
Together we are us.
Never only.

raising a son in 2023

Raising a crier - to let others
know he's not okay, to be
strong and soft. Emotions
release everyone from something.
Raising a hugger - when prompted,
to know comfort and boundaries.
Raising a listener - to hear others'
ideas at tables full of worthy mentions.
Doing my best to raise a boy
who unfolds the mold,
steps out of the usual,
brings connection and creativity
where it is needed most.

All That

You are taller, and
talk of building rockets,
somedays to California,
dancing on the moon.

You say you want to be
bigger, faster, eight.

In the fresh of my memory,
you are two weeks of love,
two months of snuggles,
two years of tickles -
and suddenly -
two more mornings until
you are all that and five.

come eat your dinner
yes, you do like broccoli
fine, chicken nuggets

acknowledgments

Thank you to my ever-supportive husband, who upon reading the first poem I'd written since 2007, said "wow, this is really good, babe." which immediately boosted my confidence and made me want to write another one. To my Tiny J, my best snuggler, my magic - thanks for knowing when mom needs a minute. Love you bb.

Thank you to my local library for being my favorite place to write. To my ADHD hyperfocus, thanks for allowing poetry to not be another short-lived hobby, but really dialing it in so this collection could become real. And lastly, to my absolutely perfect "Makes Me Wanna Write Stuff" Playlist on Spotify, thanks for keeping me creative and flowy.

thank you

Thanks for being a fan of poetry, books and words. I'm honored that you read this and hope there is a sliver of something within these words that you find comforting, relatable or hilarious. I'm currently working on my second poetry collection, so please keep in touch so we can get emotional and nostalgic together again soon.

about the author

Stephanie graduated with a BFA in Communications Design 2011 from Syracuse University and is a portrait photographer by day and writer/artist/crafter by night.

She lives in Massachusetts with her husband and son.

follow

on socials for updates and behind the scenes:

Instagram: @srk_reads
Twitter: @stephanie_rita

www.stephanierita.com

my words matter:

my ideas matter:

words i love:

things i wonder about:

ideas about life:

www.ingramcontent.com/pod-product-compliance
Lightning Source LLC
Chambersburg PA
CBHW060954120626
46557CB00003B/1159